Belief

8.3.15
With love
From
Helen +
Emma.

Belief

by

Helen Brennand

Illustrated by Emma Sykes

∞

Creative Locations Ltd.

Publishers and Illustrators

First published in 2014 by Creative Locations Ltd.

Saddleworth Business Centre
Huddersfield Road
Delph
Saddleworth
OL3 5DF

E-mail: creativelocations@hotmail.co.uk
Graphic design by Adam Hegab
Editing by Adelina Pintea
Printed in the United Kingdom
ISBN: 978-0-9926078-8-3

Author: Helen Brennand
Illustrations by Emma Sykes

For each book sold a donation will be made by the author,
Helen Brennand to the charity
Number: 1099274

PENNINE PEN
ANIMAL RESCUE

Contents

To Ed and Jane

Our hearts bound together in the timeless evermore.
Our adventure never ceases...

Acknowledgements

I hear your call and my heart beats another day! I love this feeling of living in the moment, it penetrates the search for joy and touches the centre of my soul.

I could not have found this beautiful place without those I journey with in this earthly life. My equine friends have stolen my heart forever! My love and thanks to them is wholehearted, true and everlasting. I give back to them everything that I am! As they have borne a journey to me so profound I cannot express in words.

I cherish so very deeply those who have taught me the beautiful lessons of life. My mum has taught me to love unconditionally. My dad has given me the gift of freedom. They will never know how deep my love and gratitude runs for them. They serve as teachers not only to me but to the whole world!

I send my deepest love and thanks to my wonderful husband Matthew, who saw my gifts and slowly fed them the love they needed to grow into a spring of everlasting prosperity. He was the one who saw them lying dormant, frightened to show themselves in the light of day. I honour his wisdom and thrive in the love he showers upon me and our family. He is my saviour.

My inspiration for life began as love knocked at my door. I came face to face with the power of pure love in Marilyn Heginbotham, my yoga teacher, and veterinarian Ivana Ruddock of Equine Touch Foundation. They fuelled a desire within me to search for my truth. Both are strong, loyal, pure pioneers and I am deeply grateful for the sparks they lit within me.

Showered with the most beautiful friends, I give to them love and upmost thanks. Janice Taylor, Michele Fitzpatrick, Marj Briscal and Louise Brown have supported my turbulent journey from the realisation of the book to its completion. I have felt like I have been carried upon a feather of love and kindness. Their encouragement has been life changing.

My love goes to Sarah-Jane who has been instrumental to the book coming to life, it is through her, that divine intervention put the pen in my hand. She is power and strength, a link to All that is.

My ultimate thank you and deepest love goes to my

two children, Emma and Samson.

I bow down in honour to Emma, my greatest teacher. She has taught me the greatest lessons of this life. My heart has grown in compassion, my eyes see with greater vision and wisdom as her purity and honesty have unfolded the treasures within me. I sit now and watch her grow and blossom in life's journey and I wish her all the love and joy of the world.

To my beautiful boy Samson whose journey here was short. You filled my heart so full of love. To you my lovely boy, I am eternally grateful, for you have given me more than anyone could have ever imagined possible. You are my precious gift! You sit upon a star, shining in the heavens. You are the bright light of belief. I send you all the love a mother's heart can send and I know that you do know the potential in the power of love! You my love, are this book!

Foreword

The book is about the collaboration of hearts. A story of love and development which is also possible on a grand scale when mass consciousness is directed together for one purpose. Its multifaceted nature will appeal to a wide audience. It is here the story begins for each individual.

A link back to the natural world from which we were born. My story is of love and connection with the horses and how these creatures hear our inner calls to live a full life.

The book has a powerful message to society. A vivacious story which is limitless. It is an experience which has to be shared.

1
Spirit of the horse

The only appreciation came from my heart. It bled out in floods that washed my soul drawing back the laughter that had been lost in the dark forest of life. There it stood, lingering, surrounded by a black cloak, the light was now waiting to be revealed.

They were there, standing in front of me, harnessing great majestic wisdom. They had already been there for a thousand years buried deep within a yearning paradigm of mysteries. Waiting to be released, it poured and poured. The madness ensued. The revelations became the pure unadulterated truth. How did I miss this lurking beneath my human veneer? How did I suppress it? It took these beautiful, once wild creatures to release the demons of life, to allow the shining example of love to escape to freedom.

Beneath my shield lay an untouchable softness that grew from every whim into something more than effervescence. Something that was tangible, electric and exciting. It was only these humble creatures we confine and dictate to that could reach, replenish and convert these feelings back into a life of wonderment and wisdom, far reaching any goal I had set for myself during this life.

Replenished with life's laughter and joy, dragging my heels has become a distant memory. It has all come at once. The carriages of life pass by, they offer assistance and signpost directions, courteously acknowledging our right to wave them on by. They wait patiently as the wheels of time have turned, then pass by again. Ready this time to hitch a lift, with the realisation of the journey I am about to encounter, full of excitement and promise I try to recollect when I last felt such overwhelming positivity, a knowingness that dispels any fear of embarking on a prolific journey to discovery.

I can feel the spirit of the horse rise up with me, freeing my soul every minute I am alive.

Look behind you now and leave it all there! For you can come with us, the horse and I, on our journey to freedom and love. It may sound romantic but it is a lonely path to tread at times, your safety is paramount and you have nothing to fear. All fear will be laid aside as the great God of love, the horse's soul, draws you along on your journey.

Freedom awaits! Your days of anguish banished into the light. The haze of our thought-driven reality broken and crushed into the emptiness that it is, and revealed is the intelligence of All that exists, all that is within us, all that we truly know, the unspoken word of the meaning of life uttered and whispered so peacefully among the creatures around us. They gently spread their knowing softly onto the footpaths of life, where it lies waiting to be picked up by bystanders distraught by manic society, government idiocrasy and the dematerialisation of the core fundamentals of community life; sharing and giving.

All this disappearing with every breath of life, love is boundless no more, until it is observed in something so peaceful, so strong, so dignified and quiet. Let it blow us away with its immense power, thriving vitality and overpouring generosity. Let us go in and take a look, no one is left standing, if you dare to take the challenge.

Riding high on the wave of love reminiscent of past lives, the endangered heart beats its sweet song of serenity. Alas it has come again to save the day; we all have another chance. Scrambling to reach the heights of this God-given gift we miss the true meaning, its true essence, its overwhelming power to change and reassemble our lives, it gives from nothing and takes from nothing, how virtuous. Reeling in its splendour I am spellbound. Ecstatic with euphoria I am placed in the angel's hand to witness the power of the horse's heart, as it leads me up to the skies and beyond as the mysteries unfold one by one. All I have to do is look beyond the shining grey coat, smooth and luxurious, and see beneath, the waves of gold coiled in sparkling, shining explosions of creation, gleaming crystals of power waiting to be channelled back into our hearts. Why do we find it so hard to see? Why do we suffer? It is a needless tempestuous journey that could be avoided. If only we all could see.

You are blessed, he catches your eye, it only takes a moment. Just a fragmented moment caught in the blissful second. By chance you saw it, you felt it but then it has gone. Where? Is it lost? Panicked, you try to find it but it is nowhere to be seen. Downhearted, you blame yourself as it drowns in the backwaters of rigid life as a suspect moment. Not reality. How could it be? It felt too good. Life never feels that good, does it?

The spark is lit, the search has begun, however hard you try to extinguish it. The burning flame will never die out; it was too pure a feeling to be buried under the heavy cloak of life. It was too emotional, too deep, stirring up the winds of time as it leaps around with joy. It chatters continuously until you listen and think back to the moment that you connected with such power, grace and overwhelming love. You saw into the soul of the great and the mighty, the divine power, the truth. The masks of life are so undignified, so putrid and empty. Why do they show themselves so often? Countless times I remember the chaos riddled with pointless enmity biting back at the haplessly laid plans of one's life's dreams. Longing that has no hope of expiring and coming to fruition.

How heavy, how angry and tired! Why must we do it this way? Experienced in misery we stay with it; it has become our dear friend of this material life. Give it all back now and reclaim your dignity and joy and create fulfilment of a different kind, the never ending joy that flows to you and all those around you. Have you ever witnessed this happen?

I am shaking with disbelief as the awesome projection of this love and joy is transmitted to me from the horse. The wily look of knowing grounded in time and space offers this powerful message. With no fear, no noise, the stillness grows as it beats its silent drum. I can feel it but no one can see. How can I explain? Just feel! It will all become clear. The power expounds. I cannot hold on to it anymore. I collapse bathed in the most awe inspiring substance. What can I hear? The bells of serenity ringing in my ears, my heart beats the power of its true existence, the power with the potential for new creation, for re-creation of my life. My body shudders as it is filled with the light of love, streaming through my closed eyes, sparkling with ingenuity, the ideas racing, every possibility now a probability. How can this be? How can the horse encapsulate all this mystery and divinity beneath his pure mask of beauty and strength? His open and imaginative eye speaks more than words. His language is love, he suffers in this world so dignified and upright. He takes on our shortcomings and weaknesses and carries them high upon his back. Bravely holding them up he offers us a glimpse, he is our reflection. He objects to discord and we, in our need to control, tie him down. We tie down our escape to freedom. Open your eyes and look before you! Free him and you free yourself. He is your answer.

Listen to him for he will guide you from the long lonely path of disturbance and turmoil, to the mountain spring of life, flowing and ebbing, always moving in total harmony of All that is. He shows you the only way is acceptance. Acceptance of All! From this point creation begins, flooding into your life the most deeply hidden masquerades emerge, you offer out the hand of forgiveness to yourself. You fall in love with yourself again, as a child naturally is and you feel young and exalted. The kindness of your soul spills into every cell of your physical body, replenishing and rejuvenating. The tests of time have taken their toll, but nothing can diminish the power of love and acceptance.

Spinning, whirling and turning gleefully, the admonishment coming to fruition, the founder of life solid in my heart, building the pathway to the heaven-sent missionaries. I never thought I would come this far. It is thrilling beyond all expectations. Come for a ride on this fast car of life, with its twists and turns, stopping and starting. Revel in the beauty never to be experienced in such glory and vibrant colour.

As the next man takes a gasp of ardour, he throws down the gauntlet and jumps onto the next ride. Thrilling beyond belief, he cries with joy as he is released from life's chains and his heart breathes again. Joined to his chestnut beauty for eternity the journey begins for the soul. The ecstatic scenario follows, the potential locked away for centuries bleeds out of every crevice of the human form. Nothing is impossible; every dream is now in creation. The tempestuous beast of beauty and power is now in control, leading the way to a greater life, she looks back in disbelief as he cannot keep up. She waits with patience as the veils rise up above his aching eyes and the road ahead becomes clear. Then the real journey begins, salvation for all, for this man will change a thousand men and they shall go forward and do the same. Our world now changing, reforming, crystalising into pure, beautiful, free love.

How can it be, that we have not seen this sooner? Waiting for the ride seems so futile when it is there in front of us every day, staring in our faces, a mirror of shining light that we shun for the darkness.

Look in front of you now and look for your guide hidden in the shape of the horse, magnificent and bold but humble and present. Can we turn away? Turn our backs blindly missing the generous offer. The opportunity of a lifetime is here for all to experience. Be quiet now and go within, picture your horse and see her beauty, watch her move with grace as she dances with life. Watch her passions arise with conviction as she protects her fellow comrades. She can entrance the world if we let her. She shines like a stunning nutmeg, gleaming in the sun, offering her love and wisdom freely to those who seek her out. Can we share in this freely given love from a heart so pure? We must! For it is pure love that breaks all barriers. Barriers of fear that have been laid down and passed down from the generations before us. She will take you on the journey to freedom. It will be fast and furious, everlasting in your existence.

Tried and tested by many adventurers but aborted by cruelty, as control tries to take over, the mind and ego destroy the purity of what lies within their own hearts. Icy cold, life freezes over, cutting off the blood supply to their life, their hearts rendered useless. The monotony prevails. The wind is cold and the battle of life goes on.

Listening, waiting in the winds of time the soul waits for another chance to be reunited. The horse ever-forgiving, waiting like an angel at the hands of mercy, she generously opens her heart and draws us back in. There is hope again. We must not lose the connection, stay for longer this time. Be afraid only of fear, there is nothing else to fear in this life. She will lead you to the conclusion that exists within all living things. We are safe! We are loved! We are one! Can you imagine every soul connected? Every thought shared, all love spread out to us equally. Perfection in motion.

As this expression rises up within you again, you realise you are back. You remember who you truly are, you are re-connected with your roots, your origin. Something soars within and you go beyond the mundane and see the sun! The skies! The stars! Your heart beats with joy.

Paradise awaits. Clinging to your every desire you find the courage to plant your seeds of inspiration. Germinating in rich new soil, they are ready to flourish in the woven web of nutrients needed for growth.

BELIEF

2

Washed in the waters
of the heavens

How clever this little horse is, his knowing look draws me in as he gazes at me from afar. His twinkling eye and solid features are never lost in the insecurities of our world. He exhibits bravery and calm quiet solidity amidst the chaos surrounding him. He is so sure, he knows where he is going, let us follow him and we will all survive.

Brandishing nothing but love he comes into my life

through a white cloud, luminous and bright. Tired from his journey he rests as his energies rise to do the work he has come to do. He offers his generosity daily, teaching and guiding as his armour is relinquished and his layers unfold. His teachings are of a higher kind.

Submerged in mystery we exhume the finer depths of reality, which have been caged and plunged into the darkness over time. The truth re-emerges with a vengeance, more invigorated, propelling energetically forwards towards us. The miracle of innocence projects its power of healing, speaking of the necessity to protect and honour our truth. We are heard! The Almighty shouts aloud and the doors of freedom are opened now the chariots of doom have fled.

Bring peace, take your chance and join the many who have come. Enter this chapel of light from whence forth you were sent. Be clear of this message as it is eternal, no one is turned away and everyone is forgiven.

The little, innocent, tender foal that rushes into our arms can see it all so clearly, they never lose the connection. They may have to go within to survive the unpleasantries of the human-dictated life but they are whole because they are full of forgiveness.

My bold gelding, now settled in, waits to weave his magic around me. He has en-captured my daughter, she has seen more than others believe or know. It is hard being depicted and stereotyped as not knowing, but the real truth has been seen by one so young. She is unspoilt by human laws and rulebooks and at this tender age all truth is visible. The unspoken word is so much more powerful in the heart of a child. But worry not, for those who do not see will see one day. It is all a matter of timing and the seed has been sown. A beautiful seed, waiting for the lovely warm conditions of vision and purity, comes springing out of the darkness, fearless and strong. Love radiating out to a new world, through new eyes, singing a new song.

This little horse has now succeeded in his mission, his seed sown in the heart of a child. He knows not of time and limitation. He can wait until the blooms of his essence rise in succession, multiplying from his primordial patience and love.

Can I capture this with him? Will we journey together? I believe so! As his breath changes and our eyes meet, the elective souls come together and bond. We hear each other and our hearts are exchanged, our bond never to be broken. Words do not speak of the intensity of this union. The passion and power of oneness plunged into the stillness of eternity. Belonging to such a mammoth entirety, all consuming, all knowing, here the answers to life's unanswered questions flood in, typifying the idiosyncrasies as unjust abbreviations of the world. What a waste!

Why not enter here and breathe in the peace and knowledge offered so easily? Why can't I take this into every moment of my life? I will stay here and swim with it for as long as possible.

Back into the physical reality washed in the waters of the heavens I look at him in wonderment. He is a miracle. He takes it all in his stride, not shaking and bowled over like me. He is both knowing and accepting of what is on offer to us all, this is how it should be! He is invigorated by the energy, back in his ever-present moment.

Dominated by love, he greets his shining nutmeg mare with an overflowing omnipresence all around them. I watch in awe as the spring flowers dance with them uplifted by their love for life. The air is filled with a fragrant scent of sweetness and birch. In deep reverie I hear the birds twittering, hovering in the loveliness of the moment. I am called, I am invited in to feel this invisible, all consuming, substance. I am one with them, together we run with freedom to the place of everlasting existence and serenity, I am home! Overcome with joy, I am over-shadowed by the entrail of emotion. I am embedded in a new world. Peace and ecstasy ensue!

How relieved to know it is so easily accessible, here on offer to the world. It comes in many shapes and colours but here in front of me it is offered in the shape of the horse.

The widespread momentum builds as we all gather up speed to culminate in an overflow into this everlasting harmony. It is beginning to happen and there are more followers. Belief is all you need. Belief in love, belief in yourself, belief that we are here on earth to help one another grow, expand and enjoy the experience.

Come with me now as I watch the believers together. Joined in harmony the herd meets, baying for fun and laughter of the day they race, leap and buck moving forward into righteousness. They are righting the wrongs done by man, releasing man's fears and delivering man from his weakness. They are liberated and buoyant in the morning air, freedom grips the herd, squeals of excitement and fond gestures of friendship are passed around. Lapping up the generosity I cannot but enter in, I am openly invited. I go, I shall not miss the opportunity to bask in the elemental world of the herd. Playing, teasing, befriending one another, it is so peaceful here I am blessed to be adjoined. It is with the grace of God that I have been put upon this shimmering lock of gold, pure and unseen by so many. He has let His love stream through my heart and eyes in this vision before me. Never will I feel let down again, never will I be alone for I have felt and touched the hand of God.

Before the end of my stay here on earth, I have wished for many things, but this experience is beyond all expectation. It is to be shared with all. It is never the end! Pummelling away at life is pointless, open the gate and walk on in. Accept life's gestures, they are subtle so be aware, stop and observe. There are sign posts all around, even in the dullest moment the magic waits. Retrieve, revive the senses and go beyond, enjoy the material but experience more. It is achievable, balance is the answer! No one can shun this possibility for it has been asked for in so many prayers.

We come together now and laugh! It is here for us all to see. Drop the act, uncover the masks, allow them to dissipate into obscurity, leaving only the uncovered kernel of life. Textured in silk and woven in gold, spiralling upwards to an endless, inexhaustible prism of light. Here we connect to above and beyond, the fear retracting into the darkness and dying back into the earth waiting to be reborn into the light. Now ask yourself, how do you feel? You! The creator of your new life, the re-born soul sheds its coat to reveal passion and valour so vigorous in its might, the dreams of a lifetime are alight.

Enchanting the many around you, drawing them in, each one basking in this beauty, souls begin to journey as one. Fighting their way through the beleaguered only to spread their love; diminishing the hardship and opening hearts, like fairy dust landing on closed petals, entrancing them to open. As they feel the vibration of love they let go to the blissful sounds of the melodic music, humming in every corner of their being. They open to the glorious sun and all its potential energy. Lapping up the rain soaking every drop into each stem, they strengthen and breathe in the vitality of the world. Poised now, these flowers are ready to accept the multitudes of offerings from God.

How amazing! Our animals exude all of these characteristics of the flower. When showered with love and appreciation they offer from the heart the secrets of the universe. There are tell-tale signs all around them, if only we opened our eyes.

Battling with life my friend arrives, the soul encompassed by broken chords and a dimly lit home. She is trying to escape the horrors of the mind, set alight, burning out of control from those so feared in the past. Her parents tore out the only thing that could offer them salvation. In their terrified innocence they tore out the hearts of their children. Unbeknown to them they are wringing the life out of the future.

Once again glory knocks and is there to offer a hand to the child locked away. The hand to a better world of purity and forgiveness, it arrives in the shape of a warm, harmonious loving being, wrapped in a coat betrothed to love and innocence. Recollecting past memories she sees the pain and offers the antidote. Tears are shed and love exchanged; this small pony knows no boundaries, her love and wisdom is endless. Wielding her own external armour the light shines from her. Painful memories are dissolved and humour arises through the midst of the darkness. Patient and kind, tales of woe are seen from a higher place. The allowing begins, now surging from a new abode. The fresh vitality is experienced, destiny now beckoning, for the hopes and dreams of tomorrow are now here. The inner child is released into the world, content and at peace with the past.

Reformed and reshaped she is clasped in a heart full of new beginnings. Expunction of the ever-wielding, ever turning world of defiance, she now moulds her experiences into new shapes and colours. Now crying out for poignancy rather than pretentiousness, all is well as she has now freed the ache of antiquity and a beautiful new breeze crosses the land. It is soft and gentle and its fragrance can encapsulate the world.

Matchmaking the balance to freedom can be easier than we think. Excuses are often and many. The first step is the hardest, but remember you are not alone. Tread carefully as bountiful choices are also on offer. Recall the past and wistfully let it go, sailing off into the distance. Grateful now for the lessons but more thankful for the momentary escape, this unexpected new feeling, precious and warm, can turn the fortuitous heads of many. A new spring inside the body, never rushing, experiencing every moment of beautiful fluidity and feeling. You are alive!

3
Heartache to healing

I never saw such genius! This tiny pony who entered my world, Escapism his name, is my Helen of Troy. His tender nature battered beyond belief, his cries for help echoed heartache in my whole being. His eyes were dead, emptied so young, his body in betrayal, weak without definition. This poor soul was too weak to emerge, but the spark that lay within shone from some elusive frequency. It was stronger than I had ever felt, with love and nourishment the master returned. Full of strength, a shining example of life, he never cut so quick the words of the human. So fast, so sharp we had lessons to learn. He is the laughter of life, the chase, the fun, dedicated to his job he brought many down to their deserving place. Pride seen for what it really is, egos trampled in the dust. This pony has done it many times, so simply, so transient, all in a day's work. So small this pony stands, his features so cute but he towers in strength and ingenuity, bringing us all back to the beginning, back to where we feel the ground, simplicity at its best. His love for life is a lesson to us all. Wounds deep can heal and then go on to heal our world. Suffering can turn and transform into great strength which heals and teaches, manifesting a whole new re-creation of life.

The greatest lessons are those observed in the polluted canal of life. Envisage the carnage of mass unrest buried in the collective consciousness of humankind, swirling in the murky waters and sinking deeper, being swallowed up into the abyss. It is understood by many that this is life's path for us all, detailed in minute expectation, the grief exposed for all to see, the harsh realities, unopened souls, the sinking sand of life.

Buried, we cannot breathe or swallow, suffocating in the midst of upended opportunities, all possibilities in the darkest closet. No one told us we could open this door, open it to tremendous acuity. The door is waiting to be unlocked, the moment we do the calamity is over. The never ending saga is executed before our eyes. Here we begin paddling life's streams, wading at times but always above water, always breathing in life's pure air.

Why are we taught of hardships before we have had chance to hear the lullabies that life sings to us, enchanting the birds out of the trees. They listen and fly spellbound, weaving intricately in and out of the spiralling infusion of light and energy. Reaching the heights, embracing freedom, they have tasted the God-given delights that are on offer to us all. Enraged at the deceptions and veils that are woven around us, we look for our door, our escape to re-emerge with paradise. Looking over the fence, amazed by the copper coloured angel's perception, she sees I am ready to clamber down off this uncomfortable ride and join her on the harmonious passage to eternity.

She pours out her wisdom and toiling no more, I gladly journey with her. Excited, I follow as she gently scores a pathway illuminated with colours so vivid and encapsulating I leave behind the world of judgemental bombardment and criticism. Effortlessly we connect. I hear her words of promise, they are soft and endearing. She is divine love! The depths of this horse create an ache in my heart. I feel where she has been, defeated by man, her heart wrenched out as she is parted from her soul mate. Here she entered a new union, not with man but disassociated from her earthly communion; she went within to find solace. There she stayed for many years until the gentle remembrance of potential was unlocked. We found each other just in time, her suffering became my healing. Locked together we break the boundaries and go beyond. Hurting and suffering no more, she is free to spread her gift, open to life she draws us in.

It is a mystery how, but her powers are not of our physical world. They are of the world of our true hidden potential, embedded within every living being, but lying dormant until the aroma of freedom arises.

Recollections of the past are erased, new imprints

are laid down. Awash with fervour and an intense anticipation of a new beginning, we draw our heads up out of
the sand. Oceans abound, ideas race on white waves of
tremendous power and potency. Our wildest dreams are
possible, I believe this horse has great work to do. I feel
her need to expand and evolve; her self-realisation sparks
a new desire in my evolutionary development.

Expansion, clarity and opportunity are tapping at
my door. In sheer reverence I stand before this fount of
universal understanding and accept her teachings. She
possesses the answers that unlock the heart, she gains in
love as we both gain in solidarity. Expectations are met
with revolutionary thoughts that are put into practice so
easily now. This new concept is forever rewarding and I
know that I will never return to where I have been. The
sharing of our exchange is crystalised and I look deep
within this horse's eyes, I see our future.

With chaos all around I am sitting secluded, in this
holy place. Nothing can enter but love. Hellish malevolence moves aside in trepidation to avoid the door of this
dominion. Hatred banished forever, laid to rest, emptied
from the hearts of anyone who has found and abides in

this salvation.

My grip tightens remembering this love, the same love that shines from a mother's heart to her newly born child; she would sacrifice her life if she had to, to protect this innocence in its untouched perfection. I feel this love so deeply I know I have been blessed. Thankful and so humbly grateful, I offer my hand to the gleaming tower of love, her magnificence overwhelming. As she moves towards me, she lowers her head, her touch so soft and gentle. Silent and knowing as we bask in our experience, we could stay here forever locked in eternal harmony. The softness of her breath deepens with every second that passes. We are spellbound as each of us pass, cross, touch and intertwine with the true essence of our being. Love in the shape of horse and human bound as one. Creativity restored in two earthly beings. How bright the future looks.

Fearless now in our adventure, opportunities are in abundance as we travel the distance with great speed. Another veil of darkness is removed, the light cascading is so bright and luminous, our vision expands into other dimensions.

It is rather apt that the suffering in one's life can

create a passage to greater strength and freedom of the soul. If we open to the potential within our pain we can create from the deepest depths of heartache a life bigger, more beautiful and vibrant. If only we look for the gift within it, rather than just sinking in the hum drum of everyday existence. Release now, the chains locked around your heart and see the whole in its miraculous entirety.

Ruminants forage the land, living for the moment, they are settled within the moment. Their wilderness is the home of the most amazing creatures, great and small. Never punishing themselves for free will and mistakes made, they are true to themselves to the end. We can learn from their heady departures from this life. When we assume control and take them as we wish, their souls stir, knowing an end is soon to come, but their simplicity goes beyond our contemplation. As we are engaged in our own deceit, covered in complexities we miss what these animals truly offer; knowledge and understanding far beyond this life we are living. They have far greater sight and have occupied their lives fully, taking from it all they need. We, on the other hand, without exception, have missed the whole

point, rushing, raging, angry and frustrated we engage
with misery and disappointment. Battling with our past
or alone in our future we forget to live for now. In the moment animals have lavished themselves with the riches of
our world and however small we see their takings, they are
truly enriched.

Seemingly we are all the same, how funny that we
cannot see it! Dangerously we move through life with the
possibility of missing this wonderful journey. Oblivious to
the stunning scenery, the love, the friends and compan-
ionship, we leave here as a sorry soul, unfulfilled.

The greater the need of love, the harder it is to find. It
is not found in some magazine, new design or pretentious
club, it is here for you now, it is all around. Its sweet scent
comes from within, beauty so deep and a love so strong.
You can open it up and find that your true strength shows
no bounds; captivated by life, you will only draw the best
towards you.

4
Love

Longing for love, I see my nutmeg beauty, alert and enigmatic, wondrous in all her glory, untouched by fear she is the perfect blueprint. Dazed by her brilliance and pure innocent strength, she moves with elegance and grace towards me, with long powerful strides she is balanced and free. Fearless, she stops an inch before me, eyes wide, heart free and love pours out in her tender gestures. Mocking at times she knows how to have fun. Gallant and brave she encapsulates all the great attributes of life, she plays like a child, she loves like a baby and is as free as the wind. I hear her laughter as she entices me to play, her twinkling eyes are full of promise and honesty. Her deep soft whinny talking in her dulcet tones of love reel me in. Enraptured we fly, this horse is laughter and her nurtured innocence has created a beauty words cannot describe.

Inexplicable feelings rise up within me and I climb upon her back, joined we experience the tangible energy, pure excitement unleashed, expectant of mutual expression with no misconceptions, we become one. Ever forgiving, this mare offers her creativity over and over. Her ability and athleticism obvious for all to see, she does not hide it, she displays it in all its glory, never a hesitation. Radiating her love of being, she shows off to the world all she is. Never shy or embarrassed, she projects everything we try to hide, so clever and bright, thrilled with every experience. I never want her to sample the hierarchy of my world, control, power and dominance, ego driven minds belittling their own kind. Suffering and anguish written into their faces. Bewildered, their children go on to do the same.

She will change the world! She has the potential to lead us through the intricate web we have woven and deliver us to simplicity, regardless of our past history, moving us forward towards the new regime. One that is free from wounds and punishment. Eloquence of a new genre takes its form; endless peace and prosperity, a growth never known of before, no battling or bribing, just peace, tranquillity and joy. Abundance in its purest form!

Step forward and seek your place. Do you feel something stir? Can you hear the calling? Do not leave this life before you have felt it!

Peaceful sentiment allows the richness of growth to gain momentum, like the gentle flowering bud. Our life can expunge all the fruitfulness if we steer towards the mechanical and heartless desires of a wanton existence. When the beauty of the soul is awakened, you are exonerated, reminiscent no longer as the memories are revived from our heaven-sent calling. Must we wait wistfully engaged in this confusion of the double-edged sword? Or can we join in union the two worlds we belong to?

We shall and we will. It is our destiny to accept all

and be all, we just have to find our way, the specialness of each individual surfacing as a path opens, illuminating and guiding us across that bridge. My mouth opens aghast as I realise horses are my bridge! After years of techniques, training, rules and monotony I am now released into the real world of the horse with no rules, no right or wrong, there is major upheaval as my life takes a turn. Expectant no longer of a man-made goal, I am in search of the truth, so succinctly offered in a moment. So eloquent and divine, this beautiful powerful creature had it in her grasp from the beginning of time.

Miraculous now, my days spent mirroring her, open to her wisdom I let my journey begin.

Towering above me, locks of gold and ivory packaged in lace ribbons of life, generous and giving they are offered. I accept embracing the honour bestowed upon me. How I have longed for this, abundance of love overflowing from my heart; a new river running through my body. I know there is much more to this life I have been given. Exemplary and applaudable offerings to be taken, I will do my best.

In half-light, I have begun to see, seeing from an

alternate vision than my physical eyes. Courageous in my new ideas, I suspect I am alight with God-given breath. This breath full of light and warmth can steer the world to enlightenment of the most creative kind. All singing, all dancing. Achievement in its highest form.

Pacing tenuously I stretch myself, ridding the uncourageous thoughts and debilitating beliefs of limitation, to allow the high flying bird of flight to enter a clear space. Free from the backlash of "ought" right living, clear of the unsustainable, I am prepared for freedom, alight and ready to beat my powerful wings of choice.

Fulfilment praising every action, promise all around the wonders spread among my family. They are only a heartbeat away from touching their own most inspiring imaginations.

I greet the solid table, durable hard wood edged in clear crates of colour. They blend the world into touchable objects but singularly they are matter waiting to adjoin, just as humans, but we avoid and disrupt any attempt of oneness. We fear closeness of kinship in our attempts to protect ourselves. We hide, then fade away, sometimes into the depths of despair. Hatred rears its ugly head, eating away at us internally.

We can raise our heads and feel safe to emerge; one-ness is for all and it is safe and durable. Clear the debris and it is gone forever making way for the plentiful and bountiful unions. Leave behind the escapism, living every moment to its full. Gather up speed now and let it happen.

Jesus' prophecy is spoken at last. In every heart there is a new feeling unearthed as we are taken back to the promised land. He there awaits for each and every one of us to take the path, living our lives in honour and purity. He blesses the whole. How wondrous He was as He walked this land leaving teachings of life for us all. We all die to rise again and learn our lessons of surmountable impor-tance and re-live our journey on a better path. All this can be done today, here and now if we choose to. Exactness of all attributes must be adhered to, if to succeed. The omnip-otent existence breathes life into all, but those who see feel its power. We are not here to live the lives of others or wait for another to unfold our life. We are here to create, we are the seekers of our own destiny, we as individuals must clear our own path. For it is then our light to see, not the hazy vision of our comrades.

Our determination provides the everlasting strength needed to cast away and curtail the trials of time. It is easy to blame and punish others for our own mistakes but the high and mighty fall in shame on judgement day. With our eyes wide open, the journey begins again carrying with it all the lessons. Heed the past, let go of the future and grow in the awe-inspiring present. Let it be all that we have done, we can be an example to ourselves. Change that comes from within can precede major reform outwardly. The precious diamond inwardly gleaming begins to shine out into the world, laying its translucent beams upon everything that crosses our path.

Locked in this prism of light you lift the spirits of those around, guiding thoughts back to the sentient beings they truly are. Upliftment is par for the course as subtlety takes over. Lost are the clumsy anecdotes that once mesmerised. The shift now apparent and with fervent anticipation we seek the real truth; the belief has already set in. Absolute perfection in all creation stands around us overwhelmingly so. It can be seen in varying occlusion but its promise remains the same. We have the opportunity to surrender and align, mechanically ceasing, escaping to the realms of immortality. The flow of peace takes hold. Memories and emotions lie on a calm sea bed, enigmatic journeys are now encased in their lucid veneer, all perplexities absolve.

What is left but pure love! The pure love of just being, just existing within the great cycle of expansion. Watching my horses made me see through the complexities in life, they are all self-made distractions, temptations denying us from alchemy.

Upon the throne sits no other than the elusive song of our homeland, chanted in all corners of our globe, waiting to re-unite us back to peace. Humming and vibrating through our every vessel, silent to our worldly ears. Not silent to our horse's ears because they never lost the gift, silent in word they may be but they hear more deeply. While we attune to the Machiavellian calling of the superficial material world, they are true to themselves. They feel the vein running with the song of life that they were born from. Ever seamless our two worlds are intertwined, betwixt and between. How mysterious to us but second nature them.

Ordained, my focus reveals pastures new, explained

in its sheer brilliance, shadowed no longer by my meddlesome disbeliefs, I am born into my new world in all its beauty. I relish undisputedly and in awe of such honesty and openness with myself. Like the blooming garden awash with diversity, colour and life, *au fait* with all other life, allowing, giving and sharing, enabling growth into all spectrums. Albeit the announcement is loud and clear and although I describe as metaphoric, the seamlessness in this garden of colour and kinship is as the universe intended. Giving, sharing, allowing and unifying the multi-bonding of all boundaries, a new-found richness that money cannot buy is achieved. Solutions to all our lessons, we are guided by a new light, a meaning for all. Can we not see? The heavens above are offering potential in every situation, however small.

Masters in all that we do, carrying it into eternity, expletive arrays of simplicity bring solutions to every question. We are born to find the answers, we have them locked away within us. Elevated now everything seen from a higher plane, how hard we make it! We are besieged with deals and deadlines, hurt and hardship and frontline attacks on a daily basis. Golden brown dying back, blinkered by obscurity we separate, compartmentalise every area of our life, shutting down and shunning the promise of potential. We are penned into the cage of limitation.

Fearful in this space, we lash out at disorder and punity, we cannot breathe and eventually become ill. We try to shake off the demon thoughts in a bid for freedom. Freedom that is now so deeply buried, it seems a far cry from resurrection. All sold out in our bid for this freedom just as we are about to give up, we unearth something. It is offered to us again, an insight caught in a moment. It is fleeting, but captured in a feeling so strong it cannot be ignored, it is superior to any other sense you have experienced, an echo from your homeland. Follow that feeling, it will lead to a joy and happiness that extends out into the world for all to see and share.

The deep passions re-emerge, no more excuses, the heart breathing into the whole body, beating with fervent pulses of electrical potency. Expelling reluctance and resistance, desires begin to cultivate into reality in this magic broth of ingredients. Mind, body and spirit aligned in harmony, absolute and exonerated, moving us towards supremacy. Conjugated silence above all primitive knowledge, channelling the higher calling to the opening to all attainable wisdom and knowledge. The elusive knowing within us all!

Muddled formats never succeed, horses teach us how uncoordinated we are, how incongruent our emotions and actions can be. They see and hear clearly and they can help us align to congruency, allowing us to harmonise in the world around us. It is not specialised, it is individual. Hallmarked in adjudication it is not, freedom for the soul it is! They allow us to see, forgive and let go. Free then from our suffering, we rise again to a prosperous and fulfilling life, stepping up to our challenges marching onwards and forwards.

When we are split down the middle in opposition with ourselves, we defy offers of direction and instead we invite crushing experiences into our lives, creating havoc within ourselves. Mayhem on a daily basis, cracking the whip, tell-tale signs are shown by a subduing morale. No one knows better than the horse how to find the way back. So clever, they can experience, then let go. Incessant churning of the human mind is so destructive.

The story is played over and over, rebelling, arguing

and fighting with itself. Energy all around can be used to create new beginnings. We are power sources with the most amazing aptitude to harness explosions of thought and direct them in a way of maximising our life's potential. We are the creators of our new lives! We can begin anytime by connecting and becoming one, journeying on tremendous, powerful excursions to everlasting prosperity. Seamless are these two worlds when love is the main ingredient.

5
The heart and soul
of the world

Camaraderie between the people of dominated nations infiltrates deeper and deeper into the subconscious, until submission no longer binds and the power held deep within each person is felt, forcing the hidden truths to emerge. A power so strong, a whole monolithic regime can be overturned. Truth wins out in the end! The power of peaceful thoughts leads to freedom!

The nations where terror is administered to those who seek peace, truth and tolerance, rule with the dark hand of fear. But they only have themselves to fear as the injustices done to the good will become their own self-fulfilling injustice. The bravery in the hearts of the truth-seekers know their fate and face up to fear. They access knowledge far-reaching that of any mutiny or planned sabotage. They abscond to a greater place. They are the witnesses of change, they breathe the breath of God!

Bleak midwinter hails the most beautiful storms. Eternity awakens the sleeping impulse, stirring up latent dreams. Watching mother nature hurl up her mighty sword and take with her, in her path, some of nature's most exquisite creations, we ask why? Why destroy what nature exhibited as perfection? Torn down from their glory we shed our tears. But these are those who rise again stronger and more resilient. Back-breaking experiences create warmth of soul and purity of vision. A silhouette of forgiveness embraces a new world they have taken part in creating.

Chains of fear will be released from the tyrants and belief will grow in the potent soil of truth. Uprising of a new kind this time, unlamented across the land, a vision of serenity; released are the hearts of those controlled by dictatorship, free to roam, which will suffice as their hearts are filled with gold.

Enchanted by the new world, they will shed their petals of love and share with us their gold. They are our saviours in the making!

Love binds all man's problems! Philosophers of all eras contend that the eclipse of the heart is the demonisation of all existence. To bring the light of the heart back into full glory, will see a new eclipse bringing with it transformation no earthly being can contemplate. It is with this vision of expectation, that we can all dream it in to being, the palpable, forgiving, tolerant and exonerated tomorrow. Now filled with vibrancy, exalted passions emerge within us. We move beyond ownership and control; high above we merge into exactness with our true kinship. We revolt at past habituations and offer ourselves as spirits of kindness. Temptation guises us no longer and peace is spread among us. Fastidious in this work, it is commonplace to allow and accept, this tangible generosity applaudable in the awakening of a star-studded milennia. A new path has been dug, laid in trinkets of gold and silver, it sparkles with love and light beneath the gods. Altitude makes no difference when there is peace in the heart. The heart is fundamental to our progression as a population. The warriors of the past know too well the pains of war. No one goes unharmed! The years of dilemma to our loved ones, as they are unable to move forward, blinkered by loyalty to their cherished past. They no longer have a true bearing on the future, they are lost for centuries!

On the cusp of realisation, the heart blistering from the interrogation waits to offer from its bountiful cup. As it compounds, the resonance is felt and the wounds heal akin to that of a new beginning. Triumphant! The bells ring again in the heart of the world. Up rise the nations in love not fear, a world in remission.

This pageant prophecy is a quest in its infancy. Tribulations are expectant in the new dawn, but expelled in an instant. The delusions are gone, "Hallelujah" we cry as our children are the pallbearers of this transition to the new tomorrow. Hail these children as saints and protect them, for they are our privilege to receive. Guide them from the heart to teach them strength. Forbid them to be engulfed in wars of the past. Only look to the endless peaceful future and they will mirror your love and they will be your reflection. This reflection will harm the unturned and seize their unopened hearts. Wringing out the fermented, the foul to be replaced with a consciousness alive in the midst of an amnesty, where only love will satisfy.

Make-believe this may sound, but it is to be true in our future. Helpless no longer in our old struggle to protect ourselves, we will be free to roam as our ancestors did long before legalisation of land and makeshift boundaries were put in place. We ceased to cohabit as one when we off-loaded love to stand by as witness. Our eyes closed, our soul wilted, dying in our own arms we gave up our birth-right for a nonsensical empty home, burdened with difficulties and fear. Fear which has turned upon us, and we are now too frightened to live out our true lives.

Peaceful practice subduing the outer afflictions inspire the heartfelt plea of injustice. Thorny roses perpetuate our belief of pleasure and pain. One cannot be experienced without the other, surely it is just another choice, a manifest of thought. Trembling with trepidation, we anticipate the fear before we have the chance to savour the joy.

Manoeuver yourself into a new position and release the grip on old expectations, conjure as if by magic the new script. One that is written by you! One where the fearless option is taken! Rebel against society-driven conditioned patterns and beliefs. Re-read the scriptures of old and re-new and refresh their true meaning. They will answer the calling emitted from your soul.

Take back everything wished for in a material world, it only brings with it momentary occupation of happiness. They can be enjoyed, only in balance, when the memory encompasses the bearings of its undying existence. Things can only be enjoyed insofar as is parallel to our pattern of belief. Re-lived in the physical world over and over or, in the dual reality, where it expands into a new, more fulfilling experience and sharing becomes the predominance in the experience.

We can then all help one another along our evolutionary path. With love it all becomes clear! Languishing the evermore, we sink into the arms of one another! God-protected, we move forward to another day, hearing the clasp closing on the darkness.

As intrepid explorers fully prepared for the journey

ahead, no longer bound, tied and emasculated without purpose, we shed the shell of government-run boundaries and fear-fuelled beliefs.

Feeling relief from oppression and rules, we can grow in humanity, freeing the weapons from within. Bowing down to composure, the relentlessness consumed in the loving air of suitability ordered to individuality.

Freshness facilitated in the old home of compact arduous hardship! Now extracted in denomination of a new belief, a belief tempered to clothe all in their needs. Temptation to sink backwards will no longer hold the mind, forward peaceful thinking will be the only draw.

Exhuming the ethers of free will and ordinance, the mighty will rise again! Perpetuated by the majority, time only a mask, the infrastructure of nations changed before our eyes! Coerced exchanges on the rebound like boomerangs chasing the besieger! This is a time of change!

No doubt, we can persecute ourselves daily when we are at war with ourselves. We sabotage every mere thought that had pure potential to take us to a better, freer existence. Needless to say, this pattern is so evident in every-day life, we have forgotten what our minds are really for. Examples are all around us reflecting back our jostling nature to do and get on in life. Unfortunately, the reflection paints a sad picture of the truth. Lost are the connections with our roots.

How important these lessons are! We must try to dissolve the narcissism and get a clearer picture. Soulless day to day living has created a herculean increase in disease. So many suffering with paranoia and depression, even our young generation have the highest recorded cases of anxiety. We should cry, as we are creating a generation of notoriety and they are here to make the changes of tomorrow. Support their freedom, help them make their own choices and guide them from the heart. They are blessings to us all.

Repentant in our silence, may we all begin to tread this united path together, bound by one thread reeling around the world. Transfixed is the population, as the merry dance of life hears a new tune. They listen to a melody of morality and love, with a vision to see the opportunity in giving, sharing and blessing every living thing. Equal and open to all, forgiveness is all it takes, forgive yourself and others and the freedom is truly yours.

Deliberately arguing is our greatest form of defence, distracting us from ourselves. The mechanism stopping us from progression, as we are caught in the web of pretence. We find distractions everywhere; the complications of family life, relationships, the problems because of this and that at work, the list goes on. Every reason under the sun as to why we tell ourselves we cannot change. These circular patterns revolve simultaneously in all areas of our lives, hiding from nothing but ourselves.

Purposefully we set out in our daily life. Again and again we toil losing sight of the worthy purpose which we were intended to do. We do have the choice to alter the pattern, subsequently ceasing an old way of life. The new pattern that emerges is congealed with your new thoughts creating a new wheel of life, one that draws to you all that you wished for, including the help and support you need.

Punishing yourself no longer, your growth has begun to highlight the obscurity of old patterns. The contrast helps you along with your new choices, allowing everything that comes your way, the good and the bad, seizing opportunity in both.

All experiences offer benefits and, if taken, give us

the strength and will to persevere and pursue our own truth. Just by letting go of everything and allowing!

Suppose we never suffered! Allowing would never have an opportunity to surface. When we are in the depths of despair letting go is the only doorway to survival and freedom. Other doors only lead to seclusion. Symptomatic of a belief system we usually feed a down trodden empty chasm, cultivating a harvest of negativity and lacklustre desire.

Helping the next generation by administering self-preservation of innate intention can relieve old wounds that harbour the echoes of drowning men's souls. They were delivered to teach us about the perils of mistaken identity and to remind us not to beset the nature of our journey on earth. When we become encumbered by life we are extinguishing the seed of hope. Jesus came with a gift, a teaching to us all, to ensure we tread the path that leaves no stone unturned. Embellished are the fruits of your labour when your truth is found, multiplying in victory as you break free from the cycle of misfortune.

Mirrors of our existence are all around, channelled into insanity. There are never ending pyres of hypocrisy, exploitation, analysing and regurgitating resumés of incidents of non-importance, creating whirlwinds of disturbance and turmoil throughout generations.

Expectant of very little, subterfuge of scientific ideas seems exciting, to lift the lid and look inside is worth a try. Our other option is to die in the murky waters debating what we could have done if only we were younger, richer or braver.

Doomed are those who give up on the search for their truth. Exonerated are the many who successfully adhere to the voice of their heart. Sanskrit verses appeal to our inner loyalty of inner instinct, bestowed to us all in the passage to the physical life. Touched endlessly with the heart of God we can climb any mountain on our journey here, scale the heights and more if we believe in our inner passion.

To learn and grow within, is our lesson here on earth. Internal peace creates external harmony, with an aptitude for both we can heal the seas of darkness set between the kingdoms. Looming grey clouds pushed back and the nations join in hands as they ascend to the stars, their people a superfamily! Recklessness a thing of the past, ambiguity gone, clear to hear the words of righteousness, the bells ring again clearly in the soul of the world.

Joyous, the harmonies spread like a map of love lining the land with new memories, ones of promise and understanding. Living our lives to the full, trading on nothing but love! Sanctity is a word of oath as we restore truths of old, remembering with gratitude the many who have come before us. We forsake the hardship as we are delivered into the precious sainthood of a forgotten time! Where oneness is devout and without question, given and never taken away! Just as particles join in the simplest way when there are specific occurrences. Like you and I the conditions have to be right! Incidental events concur to apprehend a prediction that would seem implausible. Memories of a prior lifetime are reignited, centuries lost in a wilderness of the never never. Ancient articles of prose come alive and reside on the dimly lit fire, waiting for the next eventuality to arise and begin burning more brightly in your home.

Accidental is none of this, forsaking your guarded intent and letting go of inhibitions supplies the fire with fuel. God can only give us what we ask for! When our desires for a peaceful life are entangled with confusion and surrounded by barriers of resistance that is what we get! Petty battles and arguments ambush our everyday lives and on a grand scale our resistance creates world wars.

The fire of prosperity will burn brightly when the fuel of desire is pure and clear! No adhesions to negativity, absolute faith in All that is and then the embers will burn brightly into eternity. Philosophically speaking it all sounds sweet! Much work needs to be done by individuals as we all have our part to play, enhancing the flavour of our lives. It is up to each and every one of us to do our work and find our truth! Stop playing out the perpetuating draining drama in our lives and herald experiences of the ultimate kind! Creation of a new world!

Tired of the old façade, I make my journey to the new land full of promise with my steeds of exquisite miraculous potential, those who can shed light on my path and open my eyes wide. Nonsensical idiosyncrasies and beleaguered persecutions are swept into the past, so far in the distance, I have left them behind. Blessed are my new eyes of clear vision and serenity. Hail these equine creatures of our world, who so trusting and social, entered our complicated world of distrust and solitude.

Upon the back of love, power and strength I ride onwards to breach the horn and sound the almighty call, to awaken the dormant desires innate in us all, reviving life from the spear of encroachment, freeing every aspect of our being and calling upon each individual to seize their opportunity for peace! Hollow no longer, filled with light, expelling the stale. Freshness emerges with growth not far behind, a life full of purpose sat upon your mighty throne won not in battle but in dignity, honour and love. How precious this is. Riding high illuminated on God's creature, surpassing all beliefs we will change the world and re-create kindness, genuine kindness that allows all. Create love of the accepting kind and passion that is free to dream the undreamed.

Horses have been all this from the beginning of time. They have watched in horror and silence retaining dignity and seclusion, waiting for us to see their light! The whole pure light, burning brightly beneath their suit of armour that has been made to fight many a man's war!

Punishments abound to the horse who showed reluctance to man's war upon himself! But no other than the horse could still offer so much, so quickly without redemption. We should look and learn at their ability to forgive wholeheartedly.

Heavenly desires are open-ended with gestures of miraculous autonomy. Believe in yourself and accept the offerings! Empty the cart of baggage, see it from the horse's point of view. He does not live by man's laws of shame, guilt and fear. The horse lives by the divine law! Extricated from any race or religion, he moves freely in acceptance of All that is. He sees the true meaning and feels the heart burning warmth of true passion. His spirit speaks to us all!

Our true abode is not that of the human form; it is of something more vast, more precious and wondrous than you can imagine. The horse may toil in this life but does not take with him the woes begotten that endangered his physical days. He breathes the glory of his endured journey and when he is released to the heavens he is vanquished, set free into paradise to roam the eternal land of beauty, spreading his wisdom and knowledge on the ancestral path. Darlings of the air they waft their wand of insight, streaming through the chinks of armour in our own horses, breaking down the barriers of resistance, revealing the blockade of temptations that disempower us day by day.

The harpsichord is heard and daunted no longer we journey on a linear path. Archetypes created in our mind, perfecting absolution, banish tremendous austerity in a cloud of dust and we gladly accept the monolith of anamnesis, remoulded now into a new beginning!

Countless bridges are crossed by this passage into the light. Conveying courage as we destroy the spurious dilemmas. Detail no longer necessary, we climb the mount to the Patriarch. Embedded scholarliness laden in omnipotence activates the pulsing temple within our hearts. An honorary gift bestowed to us all! Lying dormant, within us, without a voice until the stirring of the soul! Vibratory beyond physical comparison!

Etched twofold within us, elegant sophistication sits upon the precipice of a forgotten mantra, idly waiting the herculean edifice has the composure of a goddess. Undeniably this goddess is feared by many thought to be unyielding and uncontrollable in a society ruled by limitation and fear. She is fearless! She apprehends only her true power and potential! She is the force within us all, waiting to be awakened to fulfil our worldly desires!

Succinctly following in the footsteps of our saintly forefathers we expediate our entrance to the holy gates of wisdom. Transferred from the melancholic dreariness of wishful thinking, albeit historically pungent, you now move into the clear thinking nemesis manufactured by the soul. Exterminated are thoughts imparted to us by social conditioning. Reseeded, the magic of an empire so great, it cascades into our life, drawn by music tempered for the ears of only those who listen. Christened not by judgement or peril but by the aptitude for forgiveness and love, reigning in sanctity, jostling no longer for position or authority the war is won! Peace in absolution as foretold by the harbinger!

Abstract visions, mountains of sheer beauty encompass our heritage. Bound together by no man, but set in jewels of eliminate prejudice. I wake to realise what we have lost! Forsaking our birthright for fame and recognition; putting our ego above our hearts, we lay ourselves out for slaughter! Terrified of missing our chance to perform, we step up on the platform and act out the drama of life! A manic dance, chasing a whirlwind of chaotic events, we rush to join the party of illusion and destruction for all to witness. Tired and beaten we draw home defeated.

The saga lives on. Separate in our desires, cut off from one another, we go in search of the next episode to fill the void and the delusion goes on. Deep cracks visible, poignant accolades ostensibly retracted, ruefully our instincts try to help and offer solace. If we listen, the hand is there with offerings sensational in comparison. Expectancy is delivered upon the sincere yearning to cease the polluted backdrop of causation. The illusive needlessly penetrates our society. Stuck from generation to generation we become rigid, enveloped in abject banality.

Cloudless sunny skies alight with a beauty so rich and pervasive it mirrors the human soul, like a candle flame burning brightly amidst the calm. Poetic gestures subliminal to the naked eye are captured, a moment separated from the cynicism of a make-believe reality. Opposed to this view, we take the stance that all experiences have to be repeatable, touchable and evidential. This is limitation at its most unenviable. Restricted in this place we cease to create. We are stuck, bound to only what we can see and touch, fragments of a sky that you believe you can see are but images of illusion. How long before you see the true scenery? The hologram of life, as it pulsates through the womb of abstraction.

Devoted to aesthetics we can ponder our thoughts on brands and styling, complicated sales techniques draw us in to the hype concluding to ease our emptiness. Aspirations bought or sold only last a moment, engulfing us again with vacuous analogies, punctuated by loopholes, eagerly teasing us back to the next big thing that will save us from our misery. If that is not complicated enough we beckon this output in a tribal-like parade, encountering nothing but a dilapidated show-home consumed by consumerism. Internally uncared for and unloved, dark and dismal our true riches are going to waste. Can we leave this turnstile of rituals and go in search of the wound-healing, awe-inspiring vision of love? The potent love that can bridge the divide of body and soul, create divinity within and allow us to bask in this primordial ecstasy.

The remit can uncover any disguise. Skilfully censoring clouded amnesia, the participants on the soulful journey are locked in hierophantic unison, as the masks of deceit are left woeful and destitute brandishing the cold hardships of purgatory. Never ending, the circle goes on until we renounce our sins and let go into the arms of our calling. Carried high above us the evolutionary chant, synchronised chords of harmonising resonance sent to each and every one of us, the heartbeat of our existence beats stronger as it embraces the homecoming of its children.

Astutely associated with the connections of our birth, we enter into a trust of soulful companions in earnest, bringing about a lasting evocation necessary to see the path of illumination. Granted are those wishes to the many who dream the impossible and hold out the hand of love to all. It can be hard in this day and age where punitive rebuke is the operative response, derivatives of an institutionalised society. Thought-provoking mysteries are simple and unbiased and we are told to tread carefully. However, I would tread more carefully on the path of cynicism which culminates with a skill and dexterity in micromanaged paranoia.

Members of any institution who are led by one who condemns others in society, are poor in sight and challenged in heart. We are all led by our own light and no dictator can extinguish the power of our soul.

Hours are absorbed intellectualising every mortal thing and still we are no nearer to an answer. Aloud, dignitaries call upon us to hear their word! Although beneficial at times, of what they purport, justification cannot be witnessed. When we are mindful, we aspire to that of the greatest good. We do not need to be told how to act or co-exist, we can go within and find our true answers that bring congruency throughout our whole lives.

BELIEF

6

Intuition

Aboard Mercy we shall travel, she flies like a bird traversing the mountains of Armageddon. Submerged in luxuries of the light she entrances the heart, brought back to us in the nick of time. Quiet no longer, exacting her position, she explodes with vigour and a relentless will to enter the tombs of the world. Her traits of loyalty are sown heavily in her heritage. She abounds with sincerity and a passion so deep, she can render one speechless.

Acquittal is her niche, combined with a resurgence of the exploratory sediment lain in wait within us all. Masking nothing, she can pick out your heart's desires in a moment. Chilled trajectories embedded with confusion expound the intelligence that is reverberating back to us in an instant. Foretold of this, she can intercept the transmission and allow the warmth of the world back in, transfusing energy patterns of positivity and abundance. She finds embodied in us a champion suitable of idolising. Her will is that of an orchestrated parody, excusing us from our misdemeanours in an instant. As we relinquish the chariots of indecision and vulnerability, we offer our gratitude as the wheels are now in motion. Centring ourselves, heaven's music plays out in our heart.

Reverent in the bliss, an awakening to the stars, another apostle is born. Undertaking a new duty, he moves without fear and walks from the foot of the Almighty. He is strong and powerful, but duly respectful of his origin and the right of his fellow men and all living things upon the planet. His ego follows humbly despite earlier control and is now subservient to the purer truths. Absolution of ourselves allows this freedom.

This power resides in us all, transgression is the fatal undoing of this power within. Total unison within our whole being has the capacity of delivering the everlasting magnitude of enlightenment.

The elusive sought-after shadow deemed impossible to reach is there waiting for us. Not high upon the mountain, or beyond the vast seas, it is sitting upon your heart cherishing your entirety, lovingly watching you go about your days. It is waiting eagerly for opportunities to be re-introduced with you; to dance, to smile, to see the awe-inspiring wonders miraculously come alive in a new light, leaving the shades of grey for bursting colours, alive within a benign matrix, interacting surreptitiously amidst the coagulated corrosions of mainstream thought. Surrounded by the tragedy, we notice the Spring leap forth from the disaster and we place loyalty among the leaves, and love in the buds. Tranquillity proceeds and harmony reigns. Nonsense is the aforementioned battle and a new dexterity is achieved. A harmonising breath of the world! It is an exacting dedication for the immortal souls behind the travesty, a single union of partnership oscillating upon a framework of colour! Look not behind, but up into the heavens for mastery of this lifetime. Call upon the highest for mercy and support! Your calling heard, the chimes ring out.

Malevolence melts into the black pyres from which it came and extrudes the violation of what had leaked. Simplicity solves the puzzle again! Blooming flowers arise from the ashes filled with the purest and subtlest senses. Evoking a paradigm of extreme intensity, they envelop surrounding melancholy, turning it into sweetness for the soul. Attracted to the light, the flower senses reactions of all kinds. Triggered by intention, they sublimate into various amplifiers, receiving information and reverberating it back on a new higher frequency. Embroidered patterns embellished with supremacy and magic, curl their way through what appears to the human eye as nihility.

Extreme endeavours are made to falsify experiences which are felt in what we describe as nonexistence, but those are the times we are truly alive. We are feeling, perceiving and connecting on a higher vibration than the physical realm. Believe in these moments! They are your opportunities to substantiate what your true purpose is.

We can expend much time and energy on the more diffcult path, the path seen to many as the only road to tread, to be deemed worthy by all. But this unruly, sometimes savage path, extricates all hope and spirit. The drudgery gleans from us the child-like satisfaction in the most simple of things. We lose the gift of joy. Embittered deposits hurl from our tongues, only to rebound and hit us a little more deeply each time.

Astounded by the sudden peace that we aspire to, I am dumfounded so few have found this space. It is essential for our future generations to know their calling and stay connected, whilst living a physical life. We are the embodiment of Christ, He lives within us all. The incarnation of Christ centres around the period man struggles in, to abound with his physical duties and move forward into abundance. The simplicity of His teachings are, in essence, the fervent logic to the foremost challenging repertoire. Quietly, He spread magic upon this vast land and poured love into every stream and every stem, He told of purity in heart and mind and dreaming was our gift.

Our churches are within and can lead us day by day down the gilded path honoured in His name. No other than the inner kingdom has the spirit that dwells with the Christ, the light that awakens the world.

Catastrophic counterparts can expiate by observing the analogy, distinguished between the anthologies of love metamorphosed during remembrance. Coupled together, binding heart and soul, treasured forever beneath the holy polymer; they come to light within time-scaled perfection. Drawing high on the skyline, the beautiful exonerated movement of causation, a tapestry of delight and profound sincerity to a world surpassing enterprise.

Succinctly authenticated by the masses embowed to the germinating compendium, we will see the hearts rise above the envelope of deceit and disillusionment. Makeshift angles open up to absolute infinite possibilities. Caressing earth-bound contemporaries, salvation exhibits tranquil waters amidst a new perception. Duly considered a triumph, exacerbated by apathy bespoke in the old world, possibilities now are seen as the norm, masters of our own lives.

Temptations are a quintessential by-product, allowing us an opportunity to eradicate needy attachments. Examples exhibited in our everyday lives are the mirrors we need to acknowledge and demistify within ourselves to create these new beginnings, reflecting back to us our new world of love, peace and prosperity, growth saturated in harmony.

Metamorphosis of the whole transpires eventually as ancient wisdom penetrates the subtle layers of our body. Chemical responses resound within our makeup and separate the toxic substitutes that disenable our progress. Overtures acquiescent of the parables of Jesus, stand by openly asserting the power of truth and the clarity of vision this establishes.

The gift within you is the only possession you need in life. It can be buried deep, but always unearthed when its calling is heard. Judge no other, nor yourself! Be grateful for everything and explore the opportunities in hardship. Visualise peace in every situation and handle all your emotions with courage and love, for these are yours to accept and attend to. Responsibility for every thought and deed is our own to atone.

The calling will be heard and the doors will be opened. Every day will be a challenge, but clearly rewarding, as the gift of forgiveness pervades. The tranquillity of a new genre expediates the dissemination of love!

Sensationalism centres around man-made dramas. They all constitute the academics of denial and resistance. They hold us in the Never-never land of dissatisfaction. Disembodied from platitude, the hierarchy of destruction crumbles. The weight lifted, the heart can open and we breathe again.

Tributes to our fathers are all very well but we have to savour what is beneath the meaning of reverence. We need to feel it! Embrace and enhance the facets of this desirability. Distinction between feeling and doing is difficult because we are all more inclined to do. Feeling is epitomised as an incomprehensible medium, surpassing usefulness in society. Doing is seen as heroic, taking you to altitudes of a dynasty cast with failures! Albeit problems wash away the instinctual intellect within that can take us to a higher realm of dignity. This higher realm is one which does not coincide with the makeshift man-made boundaries. It does not pull us one way or another or trample over our best laid plans when the hierarchy decide to move the goal posts. Neither guilt nor shame revel in this higher altitude of sublimity. Negotiations cease to palpate as the exhumed generosity pulses through the veins of those assisted by sincerity.

Calculations are made to notify populations of comparable measured movements within societies. Comparisons that justify keeping us on the hamster wheel, born from statistics and legislation of the upmost fear-driven leaders. None is more just than belief and faith in the war against apartheid. It is all the same, fear of oneness, fear to let people be and be creators in their own right.

The powers of man are his passions and his creativity. Unfortunately, man renders these useless. Driven by fear, he tries to control every situation that he feels uncomfortable with. Expending much-wasted energy on revenge and coercion, to gain his safety, security and separateness, he becomes insecure. Isolated and unsafe, he witnesses a self-fulfilling prophecy which he himself created. As creators we will create regardless of sanctity. Proposed plans manifest into huge successive genesis. Heed the warning and be mindful of what you wish for!

Our journey into unmarked territory can feel dangerous, but this path has many footprints and all who follow, live to tell the tale. Unexpected manoeuvres that fall short of your usual reform are interpreted in familiar ways by those who are trapped in the vice of regularity. Unnerved by the discontent you cause to others by making changes in your life, you discriminate if your journey is worth taking! Not being everything to everyone and upsetting the applecart, can feel uneasy. You are taking a risk, but the changes you make will become applaudable and others will follow.

It only takes one who feels the calling of the soul, listens to the whispers of the heart and then traces it all back to the beginning. Rewriting the true script filled with blossoming verses, radiant words all carried upon the voice of a song sung in harmony with creation flowing into the hearts of everyone it touches. A beating heart full of divinity is sure to lift and inspire.

The sub-drama is affected by all the diversity and raises a passion driven by the soul. One by one, our layers of the conditioned life reveal themselves. Attuned to a new sensation we recognise them for what they are; nothing but fears wrapped in neat packages, layered in tinsel and ribbon. We acknowledge them and release the ties of an old attraction.

No longer the magpies searching for unworthy gold, we are now in search of the diamond, the glistening clear diamond within. Plucked from obscurity, now leading the way, the clear-cut diamond's brightness is drawn forth blinding the passageway to darkness. There is only one path now, one into the light, fringed with perfection as this dream comes to life.

In everyday life the dawn of the celestial awakening arrives. Clear upon the rainbow of distinction, the colours radiate the experience to come for this millennium. We sense the awakening of a power so mighty we all rise to be freed! With expunction of the dormant seeds within us, we sow afresh within fertile soil. We shall not regress to the haphazard autumn redress.

Sanctified, absolved from karmic address, we no longer fulfil the role of cause and effect. We are now creating anew! The solitude within brings journeys of a multi-faceted nature and serendipitous discoveries collaborate to further disengage material desire. Fortuitous treasures lie in wait within.

Fraught with anxieties, we miss the many opportunities to coexist with the miraculous mechanisms that can flavour our lives. Sweetening all our endeavours to such a degree, we can live blissfully in any situation. We can learn from and tolerate all of life's lessons and hardships as we ride through them. Eyes wide open following a shining light and driven from appreciation, we strive for the complete existence. One where love is in the driving seat and intention is the engine, geared towards kindness and service to animal and humankind. Millions upon millions move upon the path of doubt. Misaligned from belief, they cannot take the deep breath of truth which trust and peace is carried upon. Hurry to reconcile with your heart, recompense and be delivered into a just place, full of compassion and joy.

Until the day of redemption takes place, we are all held before our own immortal judge. Side by side we walk in unison before the glory of the eternal eye of truth. Set before us, a glimmer turns into the brightest light of the heavens, which eventually covers any remaining dark. Pardoned from misdemeanours, unstifled and free, we make amends. Treasured is this life! Unbespoken, natural compounds and heartfelt memories are no longer awash with the bleak tradition, but devoured now by a culmination of sincere thoughts.

Suppose we all look back on past memories with delight and gratitude for the lessons they brought. Imagine if we all took from them opportunities to improve upon ourselves with each individual taking their thoughts to a higher place! Meeting and joining with what is thought of as the impossible. Suppose we allow ourselves to experience from a wider eye that is clear, accepting and forgiving. What would our mirror reflect?

Compassion is the warrior for peace! Non-conforming creates discomfort for a while, but the luxurious seat of opportunity that lies ahead is worth the initial bumpy ride. Seclusion bypassed and trust built externally brings internal promise. The gift we are given as our rite. Healed within we have all the power to eternalise our vivid landscape.

BELIEF

7
Deity of the soul

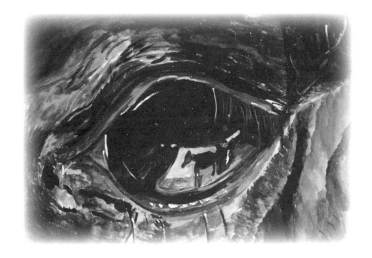

Shell-shocked generations before us, with white-washed backgrounds, the complexities of their soul's desires, diminished in the floodlights of terror. Disarmed and disillusioned, the war goes on within, until discordance is heard and the generations to come breathe love and forgiveness into all corners of existence. Reaching way beyond temporary intermediaries, it connects to a source so strong we are again aligned to our expanding evolutionary progression. Deeply filled with love, our growth is astonishing, an unrecognisable development so hastily apprehended. Hand in hand, it is dispersed and dries the lake of tears shed by our ancestors.

Chemical warfare can kill instantly or wreak havoc over decades, slowly seeping into the cells of nature. Only then do we discover we are sleeping on our own man-made protracted weapon. We kill ourselves when we kill others! We can save ourselves when we love another! We dream of togetherness with a partner, but it goes disastrously wrong. Without any point or any agenda, we lose our strongest wish. But when we love from a free heart and we love ourselves, we do not endanger losing that love because it is within us, we are love. We love without fear, without the need to control. We are drawn and carried to the right places at the right time, into emporiums of delight. Mystical it may sound, but its truth is to be experienced! This is a reality in a loving world. We are only delivered to disaster after disaster in a world run by fear.

Fleeting episodes are hypothesised as conjecture, events secondary to opposed opinions. These judgements may very well purport to be facts of the limited physical nature, but exclude the huge outstanding possibilities of what humans see as the unknown. They are closed to the most important part of life. How can we hold the whole picture if we do not stay open to every possibility? Belief is our only evolutionary hope! Expectation of the highest cause to set the examples! When creativity is at its most potent, the relentless anecdotal travesties compound into Ahimsa.

Illusions connect the consciousness to the creator! Implicit details scribed in pictures or journeys across landscapes so vivid and transparent. No wonder we confuse the parallels of physical life and eternal life! Although the evermore is far greater in design and colour combined with a deep feeling of reverence, the ambiguous nature of these parallels concludes with a feeling of rebuke to what is lost when looking with our physical eyes.

Branded or patented this experience is not! It is wholly contrived into existence by means of a God whose intention is played out within the éclat, superseded by no other, censored not. Decisions of vast importance can be deluded if we fail to look deeper. Disparaging advances into the mortal world can be discarded when we are able to envisage the sanctimonious substitute on offer.

Prejudice can carry in all forms, latitudinally and longitudinally all over the globe. But the presence, spectacularly obvious within us all, which is often misinterpreted, is the cleansing deity of the soul. She can wash upon us, sight that sees deep, within every resistance and bathe it with love. She can draw out the cynicism locked inside the stone steeped in failings and fill it with glory. She can allow us to see the Godliness within all that surrounds us and, most importantly, she can forgive us our sins. She can lift and light up our weary home and fill it with sumptuous gifts that radiate out into our world.

Bequeathed to us by our Almighty God! His everlasting promise remains absolute in perfection, imploring that the subterfuge is honestly addressed and cast aside to allow this beautiful light of purity to shine through, glowing brightly as a new dawn awakens. Shadows eaten up by its luminous velocity, gently casting shade over the wounded, it has the capacity to heal a multitude of souls. It generates an energy and love of life that expands thought processes above and beyond the mechanical understandings of the mind.

It becomes a map that journeys you to the infinite. Like the popular satellite navigation systems that guide you one step at a time until your destination has been reached, we have our own internal navigation system that leads us to fulfillment, happiness and never-ending love and joy. We can nullify excursions taken, which took us in the wrong direction down the long dark tumultuous path to disillusionment. These journeys were not registered on your navigation system. You may have disregarded your failings and discomfort on the journey, as your memory can disguise the abomination, flogging insipid desires that lacked gravitas. Wholly confounded by the inner and outer turmoil, we surrender to similarity and suffering. In still-ness we can hear our navigation systems. It is clear and calm and it does not rush you. It does not dictate a direction but offers signposts and there is always a choice.

Pleasant feelings arise and we look up out of the darkness; compounding with the light, our eyes begin to open. The shutters of obscurity become the living en-trance to a whole new world. The battlefield is empty, burgeoning new enticing fruits from thoughts of vivacious seeds, spectacular in dimension and animated into crea-tion for all to see. Triumph excels! The bespoke nature of man in his unity with himself leads to the all-encompass-ing oneness with God.

We are only endangered if we engage with thoughts that allow fear to run amok. We are eternal beings derived from a thought process and intelligence way beyond our human comprehension. Acceptance of this allows a know-ing that disrupts fear's hold on us. It sees the harmony and growth within all emotions we face in life. It helps us ac-cept all situations, not as good, bad or indifferent, but as equal unique experiences that guide us towards our com-passionate self.

My wholly owned arbitrary nuances conduct in an orchestrated fashion. Penalties arise when I am misled by determination of a thought consciousness that shields the inner perception, the ultimate unconscious knowing!

We derive splendid moments, seizing absolution, eternalising its commodity resolute, only then to bargain our saviour for the silhouette. Side-lined again! Major re-percussions for the bright light of justice and love.

Tortured beacons emanate like prolific swords of

the night. You can hear the desperate pleas of the soul. Man-made hierarchy complicates our individual evolutionary growth. Stumbling blocks are stacked against the procession, dancing towards an awakening that recognises the infidelities of the laws of man.

The feeling of sweetness in this moment of awakening is unprecedented. Our clarity within extends through our mortal eyes to see only the purity and blessedness in our activity here on earth. We see all and everything as equal and of equal importance. All boundaries line up and become seamless. We all stand together in unity, as one by one we see and feel the light, the never-ending light that offers itself into the darkest corners of the earth. Grasp this light while you have the chance, the immortal wish is yours to take.

Belittle no longer other men! Growth for each is imperative if we are to survive death. Holy attributes of remembrance of the Christ, visible by sight, enact a purpose to aid direction and enable us to experience subliminal truths beyond the realms of our physical existence. Doctrines disguise truth and the consequences can be catastrophic. Learn to listen and listen to no other than your own inner voice. Hear the calling and align to truth and love. Feel and experience sincerity in your heart and trust that your inner voice will become one with God.

Future harmony throughout the world has been prophesied! Excessive readings of the scriptures can be misinterpreted. If they are left untouched by eyes and experienced by our will, then we can truly grasp the perpetuating drive, the potential seated within us, that will enable us to see the macabre as the paltry penance our societies have had to pay. Come forth with the Lord and see His delectable offerings, His beautifully played chords that resonate through each and every one of us when we sing in the harmonious melody of love. The depths of the scriptures sing this song and it can only be felt from the sincere desire to seek freedom.

God can feel our heartfelt pleas when sent from the selfless. He hears our hearts crying for peace and sends offerings to help guide us to that discovery. Look at the meanings within your displays of emotion and you will answer your own questions. Take the hand of opportunity and change your reactions to the world around you and see your new world unfold before your clearer, freshened eyes.

Open and wide, your new vision restored by an organisa-
tion above and beyond the limitations of man. Breathe in
the deep peace and be re-energised in succession, until
each and every one of us has breathed deeply the breath
of love.

Existing parallels unbeknown to us target temptations not wholly sublime and give succour to our weak-
ening resolve. Initially we might feel it as slight irritation,
but eventually the over-pouring is all too much to bear and
we succumb to the fervent calling. An admonishment can
create unfavourable repercussions when we are attached
to earthly dramas and possessions. When we truly want
freedom, we take the reproval in good spirit and we are
thankful for the conundrum.

Cast off the night and be the light of day. Foreboding
transmutes, alight and a darkened sky becomes a kaleido-
scope of colour dancing on the nectar of salvation. Tragedy
is seen as the imaginary dream it was, that transported
us to the luminous world of pure potential. Breathe in the
warmth of spirit, rising high above the palpating unity of
the world. Generosity, overflowing from the heart is the
centre of our universe! Lesions mended by purification of

the sincere soulful message in the air, high on life, splendour so remarkable, vivid in its transparency for all to see.

How blessed are we all to have made the journey, to clear the debris and see the translucent opportunities of physical life. We are the expansion! We are destiny! We are one of the same! We all came with a message, one of love and offering. How we purge our past wrongdoings will be unique to each and every one of us. By offering our love in our individual walks of life, we can fill our lives with purity and freedom. All debts repaid!

Picture a coal mine overflowing with activity, natural resources in abundance, cleverly adapted by the earth to provide light and heat. Drawing from our source fuels to sustain life, but never replenishing, leaves a desolate ravaged starved void.

The total capacity of the internal void is immeasurable. Tenacity for the truth comes at a greater, more powerful and manageable price. Its simplicity echoes that of the merchant's prayer for sustainability, a long-lasting abundance that fills every corner. Reciting the mantras of old whilst exhuming the posthumous retractions of the generations allows us to relive our lives from the balance of giving and receiving. This takes us to enchantment, freedom and a renewed ability to find peace in every moment, whatever you may be drawn into. You become peace, you create peace, and you begin to spread peace. Harmony is your blessed gift! You have no need to control and cannot be controlled. You will never be haunted again!

Unexpected information, transmitted through the paradoxical element of our true nature transpires to resuscitate the heavenly framework from which we were born. Its deepest quest for intimacy is apparent within us! It answers when we listen and we all have the gift. The external draws are made manifest by us. Our physical lives, our free will, have turned us against ourselves and we fear to delve deep within ourselves, as we may not like what we find. But it is causation! Our inner spark, our essence is purity and goodness. Free from the muddled thinking of the world you will find generosity rather than platitude. Sorrow felt by a feeling of deprivation is lifted and a true sense of happiness and joy emerges. It is one of an everlasting nature because its source is endless in supply.

We replenish this source by our gratitude and love for All that is, then expansion occurs for all. Growth in each individual supplements those around them. Driven by a true understanding of the divine teachings helps create the world we all seek. A passion to find your truth, your true calling, necessitates freedom, empathy and belief from our physical home to allow it to shine.

Excellence in all its beauty, brimming, the cup full of life's endeavours, expunged all the weakness holding only the pure strong realisations of our existence. We tap into these inner eternal powers every day when we seek to resolve a problem. Unfortunately we allow our logic to overrule the fastest route to peaceful solutions. We hide the fear, trap it in our hearts and allow our non-feeling logic to make the decisions. This only draws to us the melancholic cry of defeat. Fear has won! We reach out to those around us but feel the divide. Entrenched by our subdivision on many levels, we need a wholehearted response to reunite mind, body and spirit.

Absolving tremendous amounts of uncertainty when we take action towards revealing our essence takes great nerve and bravery. Seeking to complete the incomplete within us is a courageous act. The clear calling you receive cannot be comprehended by the material world we exist in, but it is felt. It is a deep feeling, a feeling that cannot be satisfied by a new car or the latest designer gadget.

Retracing your footprints to the existence you were born from, embellishes with love a feeling of deep gratitude to any situation you may find yourself in. You will find the boldness in your heart to make the changes needed to set yourself onto the path illuminated to freedom. Ecstasy at this level is the highest you will find, completeness construed by a fulfilment of your individual potential, a powering tower of energy perplexed by nothing. An example of purity derived from an excellence of fervent discipline of inwardly honouring the external great masters, the growth of your own inner teacher, soars to heights you may never have thought possible.

Exuding beautiful artefacts of external youth and dexterity, you fly with your new life. You are it! You have become! You have arrived! It is time to start living and enjoying. No more escapism and hiding, execution of the dead-wood reveals the life beneath waiting to flourish in the light of day. Richly seeped in patience gilded in a delicate but strong beauty, we emerge as one soul beating together, resonating through the earth's vibrating pattern.

Counting down to the moment of complete unity, hail those brave enough to strike out and take their first step. Be guided only by love and follow only those who are love!

Here I retrace my steps and re-introduce the Horse, for the horse is my teacher, my guru, my love. I follow only those who teach unconditional love and forgiveness. That is what I find in the horse. I believe they are sent as messengers and saints to help us on the earthly path. They draw us in like beautiful butterflies fluttering in the shimmering heat on a glorious sunny day. The absolute is within every horse! Look into the eyes of the next horse you see and they will reflect your soul. Your cries can be revealed, acknowledged and healed within moments in the company of these great gods.

The love of the horse runs so deep into my soul, it can counteract the most beguiling frequencies that distract me from my heart's centre. They clear my mind of monotonous dialogue, collaborating essential beliefs of our existence. I feel the pure waters lift me into their world. The presence of the Almighty stands between me and the horse, the link to complete connectedness and wholeness. No empty voids, no missing pieces, a jigsaw puzzle complete. By the power of love here in this place, in this moment I can create my future. I used to live in the future fearing the past, now I am sitting in the most creative and awe-inspiring place on earth; I am living in the present!

I am connected to All that is, to all the potential power we are surrounded by. Never chasing life again, I will respect and cherish the gifts we are bestowed. I will write about my love of life and my love of the horse, who has been ever-present since I was a child and who has waited patiently while I caught up, never failing to guide and support me in my ever-changing life. I can speak from my heart and shout from the rooftops in my belief in life and my belief in our equine guides, for I have experienced the true capacity and potential in the heart connection of human and equine. You can only truly believe when you have the experience and only when you experience can you then believe.